Simply
Surrender

Other Titles in the *Thirty Days with a Great Spiritual Teacher* series:

ALL WILL BE WELL
Based on the Classic Spirituality of *Julian of Norwich*

GOD AWAITS YOU
Based on the Classic Spirituality of *Meister Eckhart*

LET NOTHING DISTURB YOU
A Journey to the Center of the Soul with *Teresa of Avila*

PEACE OF HEART
Based on the Life and Teachings of *Francis of Assisi*

TRUE SERENITY
Based on Thomas á Kempis' *The Imitation of Christ*

YOU SHALL NOT WANT
A Spiritual Journey Based on *The Psalms*

WHERE ONLY LOVE CAN GO
Based on *The Cloud of Unknowing*

Future titles in the series will focus on authors such as Hildegaard of Bingen, John of the Cross, Augustine, Catherine of Sienna, Brother Lawrence, and others.

Simply Surrender

Based on the Little Way of
Thérèse of Lisieux
John Kirvan

AVE MARIA PRESS Notre Dame, Indiana 46556

John Kirvan is the editor and author of several books including *The Restless Believers*, and currently lives in Southern California where he writes primarily about classical spirituality.

————————

The passages from St. Thérèse are a modern translation and paraphrase developed for meditational use from the earliest French and English editions of her writings and sayings. The refrain around which the evening prayer has been developed is from the last poem written by St. Thérèse of Lisieux.

© 1996 Quest Associates.
International Standard Book Number: 0-87793-590-4
Cover and text design Elizabeth J. French
Printed and bound in the United States of America

Library of Congress Cataloging-in-Publication Data
Kirvan, John J.
      Simply surrender : based on the Little way Thérèse of Lisieux/ John Kirvan
           p.   c.m. — (30 days with a great spiritual teacher)
      ISBN 0-87793-590-4 (paper)
      1. Thérèse, de Lisieux, Saint, 1873-1897.—Prayer—books and devotions—English. I. Bro, Bernard. Gloire et le mendiant. II. Title III. Series.
BX2179. T53K57 1996

248.3—dc20

96-19550

CIP

Contents

I realized that our Lord
does not call those who are worthy,
but those whom he will.

—Thérèse of Lisieux

Thérèse of Lisieux

Thérèse of Lisieux' story is disarmingly simple.

Born Thérèse Martin in Alençon, France in 1873, she was the youngest of five sisters, all of whom became nuns. She was only fifteen when she entered the Carmel at Lisieux where she was known as Thérèse of the Child Jesus and the Holy Face. Nine anonymous years later she was dead. There is no indication that her reputation for holiness had spread beyond the cloister walls, and except for a few missionaries with whom she exchanged letters, certainly no one but her immediate family and her Carmelite sisters knew of her existence.

But within a very few more years she was a household name, the object of an extraordinary worldwide cult. Soeur Thérèse of

Lisieux had become "The Little Flower." She was keeping her deathbed promise to spend her heaven doing good on earth. In 1925, less than thirty years after her death, she was a canonized saint of the universal church, without question the most popular and best loved saint of the twentieth century, and just as certainly an extraordinarily influential force in the spiritual lives of millions of ordinary people.

What shattered her anonymity was the publication of her autobiography, written in several stages under obedience to her religious superiors. What gave it its enormous impact was the extraordinary spiritual insight she brought to a life that was by any standard ordinary. Her story was met with the shock of recognition and its companion, the awareness of possibility. "I may not be a contemplative nun," millions could and would say, " but I do, like her, feel the pull of God. I am just one of the 'little people,' but reading Thérèse's story I know it's OK for me to contemplate being a saint . . . a little saint."

All over the world ordinary readers came to recognize, accept, and develop their potential for sanctity by adopting what Thérèse called her "little way." At its heart this "little" way of Thérèse's spirituality is driven by a powerful metaphor. *In our relationship with God we are very small children. We always will be. There is no need to be anything else.* On the contrary it is essential that we never try to be anything else.

In every other aspect of our life, self-reliance, control, worthiness will become the hallmarks of our growth. But not in our relationship with God. "The children of God as they advance in grace," Pius XII wrote fifty years after Thérèse's death, "realize ever more clearly that they will never be able to provide for themselves."

This powerful image is not some sweet by-path of Western spirituality. It is an insight that puts Thérèse of Lisieux at the very heart of Western mysticism because of its insistence that surrender, not achievement, is what the soul's life is all about.

It is a message that is always hard to understand and accept in the light of everything we have been taught to consider valuable. But in the case of Thérèse, it is made even harder for many because it is phrased in language and imagery that can be at best sentimental, and at worst mawkish.

But it would be a great mistake to let the sentimental language of the autobiography mask the steely strength of her soul and the demands of her "way." Thérèse's life and way do not consist of a sunny walk down flower-strewn paths.

Not only did she live most of her convent years in unremitting physical pain, she lived them, even on her death bed, without spiritual consolation, neither seeing nor hearing the Father whom she so loved. In one of the most poignant passages in spiritual literature she confesses: "If you were to judge by the poems I write you might think that I have been inundated with spiritual consolation, that I am a child for whom the veil of faith is almost rent asunder. But it is not a veil. It is a wall that reaches to the very heavens, shutting out the starry skies. I feel no joy, I sing only of what I wish to believe."

The little way is a hard way, but a way that is easily recognized by most of us who know that we are not among the great souls of history, and who are more used to gray days than hours spent bathed in blazing spiritual light.

Thérèse's little way appeals to us because it passes our every reality check, because it offers us spiritual ideals which are within our grasp.

How to Pray This Book

The purpose of this book is to open a gate for you, to make accessible the spiritual experience and wisdom of one of history's most important spiritual teachers, St. Thérèse of Lisieux.

This is not a book for mere reading. It invites you to meditate and pray its words on a daily basis over a period of thirty days.

It is a handbook for a spiritual journey.

Before you read the "rules" for taking this spiritual journey, remember that this book is meant to free your spirit, not confine it. If on any day the meditation does not resonate well for you, turn elsewhere to find a passage which seems to best fit the spirit of your day and your soul. Don't hesitate to repeat a day as often as you like until you feel that you have discovered what the Spirit, through the words of the author, has to say to your spirit.

Here are suggestions on one way to use this book as a cornerstone of your prayers.

As Your Day Begins

As the day begins set aside a quiet moment in a quiet place to read the meditation suggested for the day.

The passage is short. It never runs more than a couple of hundred words, but it has been carefully selected to give a spiritual focus, a spiritual center to your whole day. It is designed to remind you, as another day begins, of your own existence at a spiritual level. It is meant to put you in the presence of the spiritual master who is your companion and teacher on this journey. But most of all, the purpose of the passage is to remind you that at this moment and at every moment during this day you will be living and acting in the presence of a God who invites you continually but quietly to live in and through him.

A word of advice: read slowly. Very slowly. The meditation has been broken down into sense lines to help you do just this. Don't read just to get to the end, but to savor each part of the meditation. You never know what short phrase, what word, will trigger a response in your spirit. Give the words a chance. After all, you are not just reading this passage, you are praying it. You are establishing a mood of serenity for your whole day. What's the rush?

All Through Your Day

Immediately following the day's reading you will find a single sentence which we call a mantra, a word borrowed from the Hindu tradition.

This phrase is meant as a companion for your spirit as it moves through a busy day. Write it down on a 3" x 5" card or on the appropriate page of your daybook. Look at it as often as you can. Repeat it quietly to yourself and go on your way.

It is not meant to stop you in your tracks or to distract you from responsibilities, but simply, gently, to remind you of the presence of God and your desire to respond to this presence.

As Your Day Is Ending

This is a time for letting go of the day.

Find a quiet place and quiet your spirit. Breathe deeply. Inhale, exhale—slowly and deliberately, again and again until you feel your body let go of its tension.

Now read the evening prayer slowly, phrase by phrase. You may recognize at once that we have taken one of the most familiar evening prayers of the Christian tradition and woven into it phrases taken from the meditation with which you began your day and the mantra that has accompanied you all through your day. In this way, a simple evening prayer gathers together the spiritual character of the day that is now ending as it began—in the presence of God.

It is a time for summary and closure.

Invite God to embrace you with love and to protect you through the night.

Sleep well.

Some Other Ways to Use This Book

1. Use it any way your spirit suggests. As mentioned earlier, skip a passage that doesn't resonate for you on a given day, or repeat for a second day or even several days a passage whose richness speaks to you. The truths of a spiritual life are not absorbed in a day, or for that matter, in a lifetime. So take your time. Be patient with the Lord. Be patient with yourself.

2. Take two passages and/or their mantras—the more contrasting the better—and "bang" them together. Spend time discovering how their similarities or differences illumine your path.

3. Start a spiritual journal to record and deepen your experience of this thirty-day journey. Using either the mantra or another phrase from the reading that appeals to you, write a spiritual

account of your day, a spiritual reflection. Create your own meditation.

4. Join millions who are seeking to deepen their spiritual life by joining with others to form a small group. More and more people are doing just this to support each other in their mutual quest. Meet once a week, or at least every other week, to discuss and pray about one of the meditations. There are many books and guides available to help you make such a group effective.

Thirty Days with
Thérèse of Lisieux

Day One

❖❖❖❖❖

My Day Begins

I have always desired
to become a saint,
but in comparing myself with the saints
I have ever felt
that I am as far removed from them
as a grain of sand, trampled underfoot by the passerby,
is from the mountain
whose summit is lost in the clouds.

Instead of feeling discouraged
by such reflections,

I have concluded
that God would not inspire a wish
which could not be realized,
and that in spite of my littleness,
I might aim at being a saint.
"It is impossible," I said,
"for me to become great,
so I must bear with myself
and my many imperfections.

I will seek out a means of reaching heaven
by a little way—
very short,
very straight,
and entirely new."
We live in an age of inventions;
there are now lifts

which save us the trouble of climbing stairs.
I will try to find a lift
by which I may be raised unto God.
For I am too small
to climb the steep stairway of perfection.

In scripture I came across these words
uttered by eternal Wisdom itself:
"Whosoever is a little one,
let him come to me" (Prov 9:4).

All Through the Day

Our Father does not inspire us
to do what cannot be done.

My Day Is Ending

My loving Father,
it is only
in the deepening silence of this night
when I am here alone with you
that I am able to admit
without embarrassment
to the dream of being a saint
that you have planted in my heart.

I am, it seems to me,
the most unlikely of souls
to cherish such a dream,
and the least able to make it come true.

Only you can complete the good work

that only you could have begun in me.
Nourish my dream
however impossible it seems to me now.

Come, then, my loving Father,
you have blessed all my days;
bless me still
as this day ends
and the night begins.

Day Two

◆◆◆◆◆

My Day Begins

As a child,
without always understanding the realities of life,
I greatly admired the patriotic deeds
of the heroines of France.
I longed to do
what they had done,
especially Joan of Arc.
At the same time, young as I was,
I received what I have always considered
one of the greatest graces of my life.

Our Lord made me to understand
that the only true glory
is the glory that lasts forever,
and that to attain it
there is no necessity
to do brilliant deeds.
Rather, we should hide our good works
from the eyes of others
and even from ourselves,
so that
the "left hand knows not
what the right hand does" (Mt. 6:3).

From that moment on,
to this day,
I have felt a daring confidence
that I shall become a saint.

I do not trust to my own merits
for I have none,
I trust in him
who is virtue and holiness itself.
It is he alone
who, pleased with my poor efforts,
will raise me to himself
and by clothing me with his merits,
make me a saint.

All Through the Day

It is our Father alone
who can make us saints.

My Day Is Ending

My loving Father,
let me never forget that
if I had to depend on my merits alone
I would never—could never—be a saint.

Remind me always
that the fulfillment of the dream
you have planted in my heart
is an unearned gift.

You alone.
I do not trust to my own merits
for I have none,
I must trust in you
who are virtue and holiness itself.
You alone

can take my poor efforts
and raise me to yourself,
and by clothing me with your merits
make me a saint.

Come, then, my loving Father,
you have blessed all my days;
bless me still
as this day ends
and the night begins.

Day Three

·····

My Day Begins

God's love is made manifest
as perfectly in the simplest of souls
who welcome his grace
as in those who are the most highly privileged.

He gives himself
not just to the great,
but to the little child who knows nothing
and can utter only feeble cries,
and to the millions of souls
who have never heard his name.

I believe
that every flower created by him is beautiful,
that the brilliance of the rose
and the whiteness of the lily
do not lessen the perfume of the violet
or the sweet simplicity of the daisy.
I believe
that if all the lowly flowers wished to be roses,
nature would lose her springtime beauty,
and the fields would no longer be enameled
with lovely hues.

As the sun shines
both on the cedar and the smallest flower,
so the Divine Sun illumines each soul,
great or lowly,
and all things work together for its good,

just as in nature
the seasons are so disposed
that on the appointed day
the humblest daisy shall unfold its petals.

Our Lord has created great saints
who are the roses and the lilies of his kingdom,
but he has also created lesser ones,
simple daisies and violets growing at his feet.

His love is as manifest in the small as in the great.

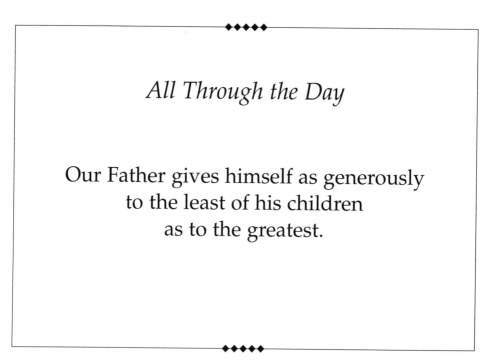

All Through the Day

Our Father gives himself as generously
to the least of his children
as to the greatest.

My Day Is Ending

Loving Father,
help me to understand
that the only saint you wish me to be
is the saint that I can be.

You give your love as generously
to the simplest of souls
who welcome your grace
as to those who are the most highly privileged.

Keep me always aware of
your gift of grace
and let me so welcome it
that your love

will be made visible
in the simplest of souls.

Come, then, my loving Father,
you have blessed all my days;
bless me still
as this day ends
and the night begins.

Day Four

◆◆◆◆◆

My Day Begins

When I found the words of wisdom
"Whosoever is a little one,
let him come to me,"
they gave me the confidence to draw near to God.
But I wondered
what was in store for a little one like me.

Wishing to know more,
I continued my search through scripture

until I found these words:
"You shall be carried at the breast
and upon the knees:
as one whom the mother caresses,
so will I comfort you."
Never have I been consoled
by words so tender and so sweet.
Your arms, my Jesus, are the lift
which will raise me even to heaven itself.
For to reach heaven I need not be great.
On the contrary I must remain little.
I must become even smaller than I am.
My God you have gone beyond my desires
and I must sing of your mercies.

You have taught me, O Lord,
from my youth.
Till now have I declared
your wonderful works,
and I shall do so
unto old age and gray hairs.

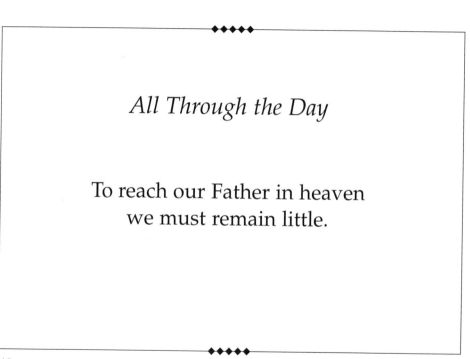

All Through the Day

To reach our Father in heaven
we must remain little.

My Day Is Ending

Loving Father,
It is the little ones
that you invite
to come to you,
to be carried at the breast,
to be supported in your arms.

And hearing your words,
my soul is filled with confidence
that there is a place in your love for me.

But it is not easy
to accept oneself as a helpless child
in a world that treasures only those
who can stand on their own two feet.

Turn my world around
so that I understand
that it is my very weakness
that is my strength.

Come, then, my loving Father,
you have blessed all my days;
bless me still
as this day ends
and the night begins.

Day Five

◆◆◆◆◆

My Day Begins

It is easy to lose heart
when we think of our imperfections.
But think of yourself as a little child
just learning to stand on her feet
yet determined to climb a flight of stairs
in order to find her mother.

Time after time,
the little child will put her tiny foot

on the first step,
and each time stumble and fall.
Do what the child does.
By practicing all the virtues
keep on lifting your foot
to climb the ladder of perfection.

But do not imagine
that you can by yourself
succeed in mounting even the first step.

God asks of you only your good will.

From the top of the ladder he looks down lovingly,
and presently,
touched by your efforts,
he will take you in his arms
to his kingdom,

never to be parted from him again.
But if you do not try
to take that first step
your stay on the ground
will indeed be a long one.

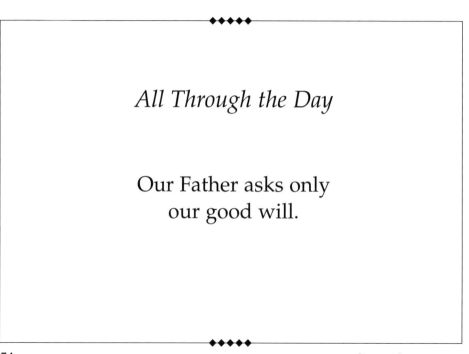

All Through the Day

Our Father asks only
our good will.

My Day Is Ending

Loving Father,
like a small child
trying to reach its parent
time after time,
I have taken my first step toward you
only to stumble and fall.

It is so easy to lose heart,
but I know that if I do not try
to take that first step
again and again,
I will never leave the ground.
But I must not imagine

that by myself I can succeed
in mounting even the first step.

My loving Father,
you ask only my good will.
Accept my poor efforts
for what they tell you of my desire,
and carry me in your arms.

Come, then, my loving Father,
you have blessed all my days;
bless me still
as this day ends
and the night begins.

Day Six

•••••

My Day Begins

If we are to attain great sanctity,
it is important
that we receive direction
right from the start.

I never forget
that since my earliest childhood
there have been voices drawing me on,
teaching me how,
in spite of my weakness,

to sing here below
the canticle of love
that I desire to sing throughout eternity.

I think about my birds.
I had a canary which sang beautifully,
and also a tiny linnet of which I was especially fond,
having adopted it straight from the nest.
From morning till night the little bird heard
only the joyous trills of the canary.
One day it tried to imitate them,
no easy task indeed for a linnet!
It was delightful
to follow the efforts of the poor little thing,
for its sweet voice found great difficulty
in accommodating itself
to the vibrant notes of its master;

but to my great surprise
the linnet's song became in time
exactly like the song of the canary.

"I bless thee Father,
because you have hidden these things
from the wise and prudent
and have revealed them to little ones."

You have deigned to stoop down
and instruct me gently
in the secrets of your love.

All Through the Day

Instruct us, Father, gently
in the secrets of your love.

SIMPLY SURRENDER

My Day Is Ending

Loving Father,
make me a willing student
of your ways.
Teach me to be as patient with myself
as you are
in my poor imitations
of the saint you call me to be.
Instruct me gently,
for I am one of your little ones.

Bless me, Father;
reveal to me
what so often remains hidden
from the wise and prudent.

It is difficult for me
in my weakness
to offer you more than
a poor imitation of
of the love
I desire to feel.

Come, then, my loving Father,
you have blessed all my days;
bless me still
as this day ends
and the night begins.

Day Seven

◆◆◆◆◆

My Day Begins

I cannot understand
those souls who are afraid
of such an affectionate friend.
Sometimes when I read books
in which perfection is put before us
with our goal obstructed by a thousand obstacles,
my poor little head is quickly fatigued.
I close the learned treatise
which tires my brain
and dries up my heart,

and I turn to the sacred scriptures.
Then all becomes clear.

A single word opens up infinite vistas,
perfection seems easy,
and I see that it is enough
to acknowledge one's own nothingness
and surrender oneself like a child
to God's affectionate arms.
Leaving to great and lofty minds
the beautiful books that I cannot understand,
still less put in practice,
I rejoice in my littleness,
because only little children
and those who are like them
shall be admitted to the heavenly banquet.

Fortunately, there are many mansions
in my Father's house.
If there were only
those seemingly incomprehensible mansions
with their baffling approaches,
I should never enter there.

My own way is
all confidence and love.

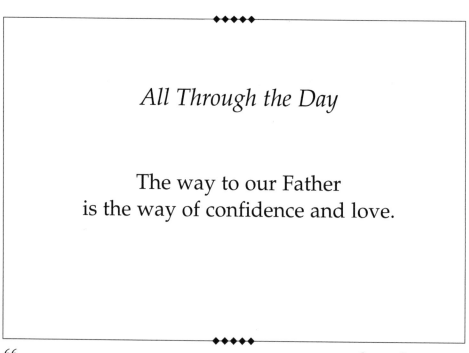

All Through the Day

The way to our Father
is the way of confidence and love.

My Day Is Ending

Loving Father,
if I am not to lose courage
on the way
I need always to remember that
there are many mansions in your house.
If there was room only
for great saints and scholars,
I could never enter your house.

With Thérèse
let my way be one that is
all confidence and love.
Let me never forget
that it is enough
to acknowledge my own nothingness

and surrender myself like a child
into your affectionate arms.

Come, then, my loving Father,
you have blessed all my days;
bless me still
as this day ends
and the night begins.

Day Eight

My Day Begins

When I was still very young,
a teacher asked me
what I did on holidays when I was home.
I answered timidly,
"I often hide in a corner of my room,
where I can shut myself in with bed curtains,
and then I think."

"But what do you think about?"
she said laughingly.

"I think about God,
about the shortness of life,
about eternity—
in a word, I think."
I know now
that I was even then
really engaged in mental prayer
under the guidance of a gentle Master.
I know that
"The kingdom of God is within us,"
that Our Master
has no need of book or teacher
to instruct our soul.
The Teacher of teachers
instructs without sound of words,
and though I have never heard him speak,

I know that he is within me,
always guiding and inspiring me;
and just when I need them,
lights, hitherto unseen, break in upon me.
Now it is, as a rule,
not during prayer
that this happens,
but in the midst of my daily duties.

All Through the Day

The kingdom of our Father
is within us.

My Day Is Ending

Loving Father,
I know that
your kingdom is within me,
that in the end
I have no need of book or teacher
to instruct my soul.
For you, the Teacher of teachers,
will instruct me
without sound of words.
Though I may never hear you speak,
I know that you are within me,
always guiding and inspiring me.
I need only to stop from time to time

and think about you,
about the shortness of my life,
about eternity.
Let there always be time for you.

Come, then, my loving Father,
you have blessed all my days;
bless me still
as this day ends
and the night begins.

Day Nine

❖❖❖❖❖

My Day Begins

All souls cannot be alike.
They must differ
so that each divine perfection
may receive its due.
To me he has shown his infinite mercy
and in this resplendent mirror
I contemplate his other attributes.
There each appears radiant with love—
his justice perhaps more than the rest.

I know that God is infinitely just
but his very justice
that terrifies so many souls
is the source of all my confidence and joy.

His justice takes into account
our good intentions
And gives to virtue its reward.
What a sweet joy
to remember that our Lord is just—
that he takes into account our weakness
and knows well the frailty of our nature.

It is because he is just.
"He is compassionate and merciful,
long suffering, and generous in his mercy.
He remembers that we are dust.

As a father
has compassion on his children,
so has the Lord
compassion on those
that fear him."
What then, need I fear?
Will not the God of infinite justice,
who deigns to pardon lovingly
the sins of the prodigal son,
be also just to me?
Therefore I hope for as much
from the justice of the Lord as
from his mercy.

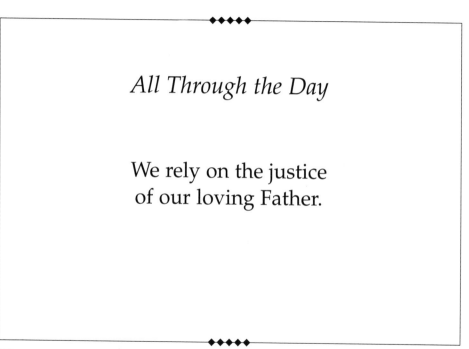

All Through the Day

We rely on the justice
of our loving Father.

My Day Is Ending

Loving Father,
I know that you are infinitely just,
but let your very justice
that terrifies so many souls
be the source of all my confidence and joy.

Your justice takes into account
my good intentions
as well as my weakness
for you know well
the frailty of my nature.

What then need I fear?
Will not you, the God of infinite justice,
who deigns to pardon lovingly

the sins of the prodigal son,
be also just to me?
Therefore I hope for as much from your justice
as from your mercy.

Come, then, my loving Father,
you have blessed all my days;
bless me still
as this day ends
and the night begins.

Day Ten

•••••

My Day Begins

To stay little
we must recognize our own insignificance
and expect everything from the goodness of God.

Every parent tries to give
a child everything it needs,
but when we have grown up
our parents no longer feed us
but tell us to find work and earn a living.

I do not want to hear this from my Father
for I am incapable of earning my living—

of earning life eternal.
So I am content to do only what a child can do,
the little things that please almighty God.

Again, being a little child
means not attributing to ourselves
any virtues we may possess.
On the contrary,
it means recognizing the fact
that God places the treasury of his virtue
in our childish hands
for us to use as we need it.
But it remains his treasure, his gift.

Finally, staying little
means not losing courage
when we tumble,

for we are too small
to suffer serious injury.
We must stay little
in order to make quick progress
along the path of divine love.

You will be able to say with John of the Cross:
"By stooping so low
I mounted so high
that I was able to reach my goal."

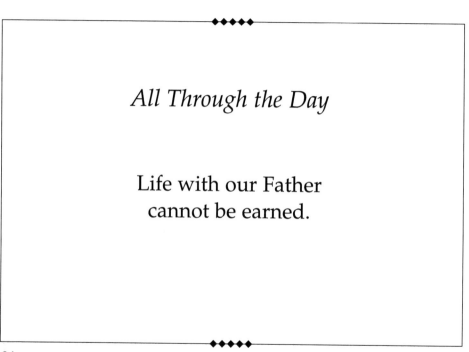

All Through the Day

Life with our Father
cannot be earned.

My Day Is Ending

Loving Father,
I have been taught all my life
that my worth depends on my earning my way.
But I cannot earn your love;
I cannot earn a life with you.
Rather I must recognize
my own helplessness
and expect everything from your goodness.

Whatever virtues I may possess
are a gift from you,
a treasury that you put at my disposal
to be used as I need them.
But they remain your treasure, your gift.

Only by becoming a child again
can I stand tall enough
to reach my goal.

Come, then, my loving Father,
you have blessed all my days;
bless me still
as this day ends
and the night begins.

Day Eleven

◆◆◆◆◆

My Day Begins

The lowest place
is the only spot on earth
which is not open to envy.
Here alone there is neither vanity
nor afflictions of the spirit.
Yet "the way of a man
is not his own,"
and sometimes
we find ourselves wishing for
things that dazzle.

When that happens
there is nothing to do
but to take our stand
among the imperfect
and look upon ourselves
as very little souls
who at every instant
need to be upheld
by the goodness of God.

The very moment he sees us,
fully convinced of our nothingness,
and hears us cry out:
"My foot stumbles, Lord,
but your mercy
is my strength,"
He reaches out his hand to us.

Should we attempt great things, however,
even when we are motivated by zeal,
he deserts us.
So all we have to do
is humble ourselves,
to bear with meekness,
our imperfections.

Herein lies
the secret for us
of true holiness.

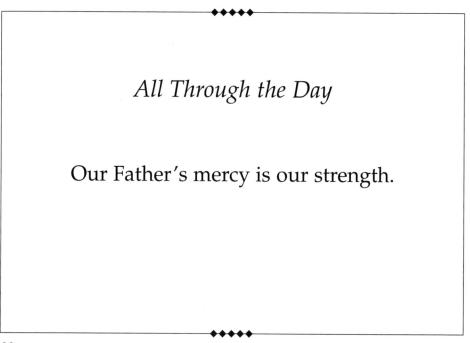

All Through the Day

Our Father's mercy is our strength.

My Day Is Ending

Loving Father,
let me take my stand
among the imperfect
and look upon myself
as a very little soul
who at every instant
needs to be upheld
by your goodness.

Let me always bear
my imperfections with meekness,
for herein,
for me,
lies true holiness.

The very moment you see me
fully convinced of my nothingness,
and hear me cry out:
"My foot stumbles, Lord,
but your mercy
is my strength,"
reach out your hand to me.

Come, then, my loving Father,
you have blessed all my days;
bless me still
as this day ends
and the night begins.

Day Twelve

◆◆◆◆◆

My Day Begins

To be a spouse of Jesus,
to be a daughter of Carmel
and in union with God
to be the mother of souls—
should not all this be enough for me?

In the Book of Life are written the deeds of the saints.
Each one of these deeds
I would like to accomplish for God.
What answer is there to folly such as this?

Is there on earth a soul more feeble than mine?
As I meditated on the Mystical Body of Christ,
I could not recognize myself among any of its members.
Or was it rather
that I wished to recognize myself in all?
Charity gave me the key to my vocation.

I understood that since the Body of Christ
is made up of different members,
it could not lack the most necessary
and most nobly endowed of all the bodily organs.
I understood that the Body of Christ has a heart—
a heart on fire with love.
I saw too that love imparts life
to all its members,
so that should love ever fail,

apostles would no longer preach the gospel,
and martyrs would no longer shed their blood.
Finally I realized that love includes every vocation,
that love is all things,
that love is eternal,
reaching down through the ages
and stretching to the uttermost parts of the earth.
I have found my vocation at last—my vocation is love!
I have found my place in the bosom of the Body of Christ.
In his body I shall be love.

Thus I shall be all things and my dreams will be fulfilled.
We cannot all be apostles, prophets,
or doctors of the church.
The Body of Christ
is composed of different members;
the eye cannot also be the hand.

All Through the Day

Our Father calls us to love.

My Day Is Ending

Loving Father,
the Body of Christ
is composed of different members.
We cannot all be apostles, prophets,
or doctors of the church.
Certainly I cannot.
But I can be what you call me to be.

Call me then
as you called Thérèse,
to be love.

Thus I shall be all things,
for love includes every vocation.
Love is all things;

love is eternal.
It reaches down through the ages
and stretches to the uttermost parts of the earth.

My vocation is at last found,
and my dreams fulfilled.

Come, then, my loving Father,
you have blessed all my days;
bless me still
as this day ends
and the night begins.

Day Thirteen

◆◆◆◆◆

My Day Begins

When our Lord
gave us his new commandment,
his own commandment,
he not only required us
to love our neighbors
as ourselves,
but would have us love them
even as he loves them,
as he will
until the end of time.

My Jesus,
you never ask
what is impossible.
You know better than I
how frail and imperfect I am.
You know that
I shall never love others
as you have loved them,
unless you love them yourself
within me.

It is because you desire
to grant me this grace,
that you have given us
a new commandment,
one that I cherish dearly.
It proves to me

that it is your will to love in me
all those you bid me to love.
When I show charity to others,
I know that it is Jesus
who is acting within me,
and the more closely I am united to him
the more truly I love others.

All Through the Day

When we love one another,
our Father is acting within us.

My Day Is Ending

Loving Father,
you have commanded me to love others
as you love them.
You never ask
what is impossible.
But you know better than I
how frail and imperfect I am.
You know that
I shall never be able to fulfill
your commandment to love others
as you have loved them,
unless you love them yourself
within me.
When I show charity to others,

let me not forget that you
are acting within me,
and the more closely I am united to you
the more truly I love others.

Come, then, my loving Father,
you have blessed all my days;
bless me still
as this day ends
and the night begins.

Day Fourteen

••••••

My Day Begins

We have our natural likes and dislikes.
We feel drawn to one person
and may be tempted to go out of our way
to avoid another.
Well, our Lord tells me
that this last is the person
I must love and pray for.
"If you love only those that love you,
what thanks are to you?
For sinners also love those that love them."

Nor is it enough to love;
we must prove our love.
We take a natural delight in pleasing our friends,
but this is not charity.
Even sinners do the same.

We cannot always, indeed,
carry out to the letter
the words of the gospel,
for occasions arise
when we are compelled to refuse a request.
Yet when charity has taken deep root in our soul,
it shows itself outwardly.
There is always a way of refusing so graciously
that the refusal affords as much pleasure
as the gift itself.

We must not avoid the importunate.
Nor should we be kind
for the sake of being considered so,
nor in the hope that our kindness will be returned.
"Do good hoping for nothing thereby,
and your reward shall be great."

The divine precepts
do assuredly run counter to our natural inclinations,
and without the help of grace
it would be impossible
to understand them,
much less put them into practice.

All Through the Day

Do good, hoping for nothing thereby,
and your reward shall be great.

My Day Is Ending

Loving Father,
your precepts most certainly
run counter to my natural inclinations,
and without the help of grace
it would be impossible
for me to understand them,
much less put them into practice.

My inclination is
to love those who love me.
But even the most sinful among us
does this much.
My inclination is to be kind
for the sake of being considered so.

But you ask more.

I am inclined to be kind
in the hope that my kindness will be returned.
But you tell me
that I must do good,
hoping for no return.

Come, then, my loving Father,
you have been kind to me all my days;
bless me still
as this day ends
and the night begins.

Day Fifteen

_{◆◆◆◆◆}

My Day Begins

If you were to judge
by the poems that I write
you might think
that I have been inundated with spiritual consolation,
that I am a child
for whom the veil of faith is almost rent asunder.

But it is not a veil.
It is a wall
which reaches to the very heavens,
shutting out the starry skies.

I cannot exaggerate the night of my soul.
When I sing in my verses of the happiness of heaven
and the eternal possession of God,
I feel no joy,
I sing only of what I wish to believe.

Sometimes, I confess, a feeble ray of sunshine
penetrates my dark night
and brings me a moment of relief,
but after it has passed,
the remembrance of it,
instead of consoling me,
makes the blackness seem denser still.
One must pass through the tunnel
to understand how black is its darkness.

Yet I have never experienced more fully

the sweetness and mercy of our Lord.
He does not send so heavy a cross,
when it would discourage us,
but chooses a time when we are best able to bear it.

There is a land to which I have aspired
since my childhood,
and the king of that sunlit land
has dwelt among us in the land of darkness
for three and thirty years,
even though in our darkness
we did not understand
that he was the Light of the World.

All Through the Day

Even in the darkness,
let us sing to the Father
of what we wish to believe.

My Day Is Ending

Loving Father,
no more than Thérèse can I expect
days flooded with sunshine
and unbroken joy in your presence.
There will be as much darkness as light,
perhaps even more.
All my desires,
all my efforts,
will be no substitute
for the unrewarded faith
that alone can uncover your presence
on the darkest days.
I will have to come to you
feeling no joy,

dependent on what faith tells me is true.

Come, then, Light of the World
dwell with me
in the land that is so often dark.
Breach the wall
which seems to reach to the very heavens
shutting out the starry skies.

Come, then, my loving Father,
you have blessed all my days;
bless me still
as this dark day ends
and the night begins.

Day Sixteen

My Day Begins

When everything looks black,
it is indeed a heavy cross.
But you are not always to blame
when this happens.
Do everything to detach yourself
from passing cares,
and then rest assured
that your Father will do the rest.
He will not allow you
to fall into the abyss.

Be of good courage.
Do not be afraid of your little failures.
It is folly to pass your time on earth
fretting over little things
that you cannot change.
Instead rest in the arms of your Father.

Do not be afraid of the dark
nor complain
that you cannot see him
who carries you in his arms.

Trust.

The dark will lose its terrors
and before long, peace,
even joy,
will return once more.

Do not be afraid
to tell Jesus that you love him,
even when you do not actually feel that love.

In this way you will compel him
to come to you
and carry you,
like the child you will always be,
too weak to walk on your own.

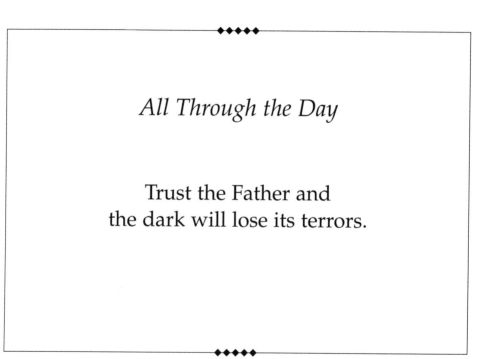

All Through the Day

Trust the Father and
the dark will lose its terrors.

My Day Is Ending

Loving Father,
it is folly, I know,
to pass my time on earth
fretting over little things
that I cannot change.
I should instead rest in your arms.

Help me then
not to be afraid of the dark,
not to complain
that I cannot see you,
you on whom I totally depend.

Strip the dark of its terrors
so that before long, peace,

if not joy,
will return to my soul
once more.

Come, even now, my loving Father,
you have blessed all my days;
and bless me
as this day ends
and the night begins.

Day Seventeen

◆◆◆◆◆

My Day Begins

From my childhood
I have had the conviction that I should one day
be released from this land of darkness,
that I should one day
enter your kingdom of light.

I have believed it, not only
because of what I have been taught,
but also because
the deepest and most secret longings of my heart

have assured me that there is
another more beautiful country,
an abiding dwelling-place in store for me.
But now I am surrounded
by a deep fog that finds its way into my very soul,
and so blinds me
that I can no longer see
the lovely picture of my promised home.
It has all faded away.

It seems to me that the darkness itself has a voice
that mocks my belief:
"You dream of a land of light and fragrance.
You believe that the Creator of these wonders
will be for ever yours.
You think to escape
from the mists in which you now languish.

Hope on! Hope on!
Look forward to death!
It will give you not what you hope for,
but a night that is darker still,
a night of utter nothingness."
But still I say:
"O Lord, you have given me a delight in your deeds
and I am content to sacrifice during this life
all joyous thoughts of the home
that awaits me."

All Through the Day

Hope in our Father
will not be in vain.

SIMPLY SURRENDER

My Day Is Ending

Loving Father,
I know that I look foolish,
sometimes even to myself,
for the hope that I place in you,
for the dream I cherish,
of light and life at the end of this darkness.

But I go on believing in you.
I go on believing that there is
another more beautiful country,
an abiding dwelling-place in your presence
in store for me.

Support, I pray you,
these deepest and most secret longings of my heart,

and dispel the deep fog
that too often
finds its way into my very soul,
and so blinds me
that I can no longer see you.

Come, then, my loving Father,
you have blessed all my days;
bless me still
as this day ends
and the night begins.

Day Eighteen

◆◆◆◆◆

My Day Begins

How little we understand the love of Jesus.

It is only natural
to dread the judgment of God.
But it is needless.
Whenever we return to our Lord,
he blots out our sins from his memory.
He loves us even more tenderly
than before we fell.
He soon forgets our infidelities.

He sees
only our longing after perfection,
and the sight rejoices his heart.
So do not be afraid that your Father
is put off at the sight of your many failings.

Our Lord has every imaginable perfection
but—dare I say it—
he has one great handicap.

When it comes to his love for us,
he is blind.
His heart thrills with joy
when he has to deal
with those who truly love,
and who, after each little fault,

fling themselves into his arms,
imploring forgiveness.

He says to his angels
what the prodigal's father said to his servants:
"Put a ring upon his finger,
and let us rejoice."

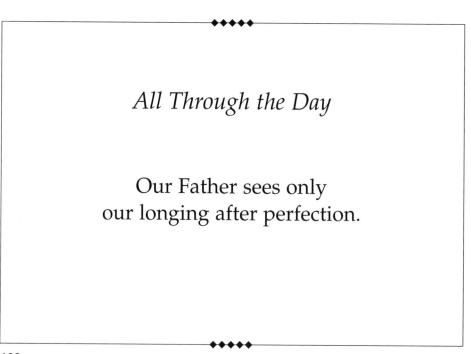

All Through the Day

Our Father sees only
our longing after perfection.

My Day Is Ending

Loving Father,
how little I understand your love.

It is only natural
to dread your judgment.
But it is needless.
Whenever I return to you,
my loving Father,
you blot out my sins from your memory.
You love me even more tenderly
than before.
I must never forget
that I need not be afraid,
that you are not put off

at the sight of my many failings.
When after each fault
I come to you
to implore forgiveness,
you say to your angels
what the prodigal's father said to his servants:
"Put a ring upon his finger,
and let us rejoice."

Come, then, my loving Father,
who have forgiven me all my days;
forgive me still
as this day ends
and the night begins.

Day Nineteen

My Day Begins

All around us
the merciful love of God
is ignored and rejected.
Those on whom our Lord
would lavish his love
turn to the things of this world
and seek to find their happiness
in the passing moment.

O, my God,
must that love which is disdained
stay in your heart?

It seems to me
that if you were to find souls
offering themselves as a holocaust to your love,
you would consume them rapidly
in the fire of that love,
and would be pleased to set free
those flames of infinite tenderness
that await us in your heart.

If your justice needs to be satisfied on earth,
how much more your merciful love?

O Jesus,
permit me to be the victim of your mercy.
Consume me
in the holocaust of your divine love.

God answered my prayer.
Since that day, love has surrounded and penetrated me.
At every moment
God's merciful love renews and purifies me.
If all weak and imperfect souls such as mine
felt as I do,
none would despair of reaching the summit of love
since Jesus does not look for deeds,
but only for gratitude and self-surrender.
This is all our Lord requires of us.
He wants our love.

All Through the Day

At every moment
our Father's merciful love is
renewing and purifying us.

My Day Is Ending

Loving Father,
even weak and imperfect souls such as mine
need never despair of reaching
the summit of love.

You do not look for deeds,
but only for gratitude and self-surrender.
This is all you require of me.
You ask that I return your merciful love
that, at every moment,
is renewing and purifying me.

All around me
your merciful love
is ignored and rejected.

Those on whom you would lavish your love
turn to the things of this world
and seek to find their happiness
in the passing moment.

Too often I am one of them.

Come, then, my loving Father,
you have blessed all my days;
bless me still
as this day ends
and the night begins.

Day Twenty

◆◆◆◆◆

My Day Begins

God, in his infinite mercy
has given me a clear insight
into the deep mysteries of charity.
If only I could express what I know,
you would hear heavenly music;
but I can only stammer like a child,
and if the words of Jesus were not my support,
I would beg off and hold my peace.

I am a very little soul
who can only offer to God very little things.

My utter helplessness no longer distresses me;
I even glory in it,
and expect each day
to reveal some fresh imperfection.
Indeed these insights on my nothingness
do me more good than insights on matters of faith.
Remembering that
Charity covers a multitude of sins,
I draw upon the rich mine
which our Savior has opened for us in the gospels.
I search their depths
and call out with the psalmist:
"I have run in the way of your commandments
since you have enlarged my heart."

Love alone can expand our heart.

"Jesus, ever since the sweet flame of charity
has consumed me,
I have run with delight
in the way of your new commandment.
Let me run joyfully
until that glorious day
when I shall follow you
to that boundless realm
singing a new canticle—
the canticle of love."

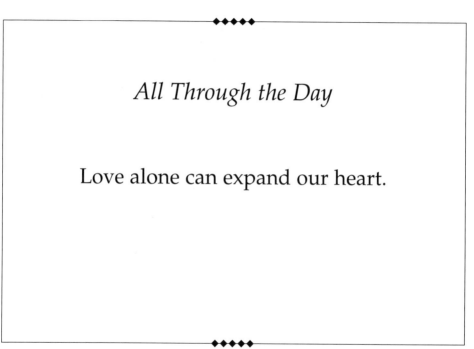

All Through the Day

Love alone can expand our heart.

My Day Is Ending

Loving Father,
my utter helplessness
still distresses me;
I am not like Thérèse who could glory in it,
expecting each day
to reveal some fresh imperfection.

But let me remember as she did
that charity covers a multitude of sins,
that love,
and love alone,
can expand our hearts.

Let me commit myself then,
to your new commandment;

let me at least try
to love others as you have loved them.
Let love govern my days
and set the course for my heart.

Come, then, my loving Father,
you have blessed all my days;
bless me still
as this day ends
and the night begins.

Day Twenty-One

•••••

My Day Begins

Do not think
that I am overwhelmed
with consolation.
Far from it.
My joy consists
in being deprived of all joy here on earth.
Jesus does not guide me openly.
I neither see nor hear him.
Nor is it through books that I learn,
for I do not understand what I read.

Yet at times I am consoled by some chance words.

One evening, for example,
after a meditation passed in utter dryness,
I read these words
spoken by our Lord to St. Margaret Mary:
"Here is the Master I give thee,
He will teach all that thou should do.
I wish to make thee read in the Book of Life
wherein is contained the science of love."

I wish for no other knowledge,
and like the spouse
in the Canticle of Canticles,
"having given up
all the substance of my house for love,
I reckon it as nothing."

I understand clearly
that it is through love alone
that we can become pleasing to God,
and my sole ambition is to acquire it.

And Jesus has deigned to point out to me
that the only way which leads to Love's divine furnace
is the way of self-surrender.
It is like the confidence of the little child
who sleeps without fear in its father's arms.
Through the mouth of Solomon
the Holy Spirit has told us:
"Whosoever is a little one,
let him come unto me.
To the one who is little
mercy is granted."

All Through the Day

It is surrendering to our Father
that leads to love.

My Day Is Ending

Loving Father,
I understand clearly
that it is through love alone
that I can become pleasing to you.
Let my sole ambition be
to acquire and grow in that saving love.

May I understand with Thérèse
that the only way which leads to such love
is the way of self-surrender,
It is like the confidence of the little child
who sleeps without fear in its father's arms.

I have read:
"Whosoever is a little one,

let him come unto me."
And I have read:
"To the one who is little
mercy is granted."

I place my hope in you.

Come, then, my loving Father,
you have blessed all my days;
bless me still
as this day ends
and the night begins.

Day Twenty-Two

◆◆◆◆◆

My Day Begins

Far from feeling consoled,
I spend my retreats in a state of spiritual desolation—
seemingly abandoned by God.
Jesus sleeps!
But how rarely will souls
allow him to sleep in peace!
Wearied with making continual advances,
our good Master readily avails himself
of the repose I offer him,
and in all probability

will sleep on
until my great and everlasting retreat.
This, however, rejoices rather than grieves me.
I should not, I suppose,
rejoice in my dryness of soul,
but rather attribute it
to my want of fervor and fidelity.
I suppose I should be distressed
that I so often
fall asleep during meditation
and thanksgiving after holy communion,
but I reflect
that little children,
asleep or awake,
are equally dear to their parents;
that to perform operations

doctors put their patients to sleep;
and finally that
"The Lord knows our frame.
he remembers
that we are but dust."

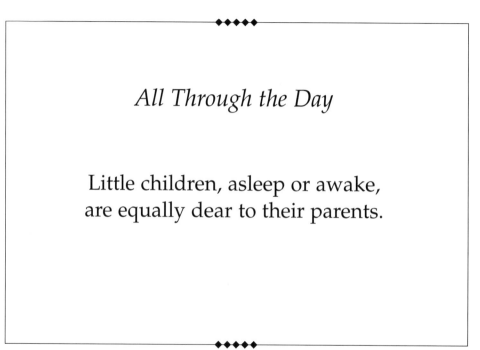

All Through the Day

Little children, asleep or awake,
are equally dear to their parents.

SIMPLY SURRENDER

My Day Is Ending

Loving Father,
you are better than I am
at remembering my frailty,
that I have come from dust.

Let me not forget who I am
and from where I have come.

Let me not go on expecting more of myself,
more of my humanity, than you do.

If my soul seems to be
forever dry when I hope for passion,
if despite my best efforts
I still fall asleep in your presence,
if I feel nothing but spiritual desolation

as though I have been abandoned by you,
let me remember what Thérèse never forgot:
that little children,
asleep or awake,
are equally dear to their parents.

Come, then, my loving Father,
you have blessed all my days;
bless me still
as this day ends
and the night begins.

Day Twenty-Three

◆◆◆◆◆

My Day Begins

Let us suppose that the son of a very clever doctor,
stumbling over a stone in the road,
falls and breaks his leg.
His father hastens to his aid,
and binds up the fractured limb
with all the skill at his command.
When cured, the son
shows the utmost gratitude,
with good reason.
But on the other hand,

suppose that the father,
knowing that a large stone lies on his son's path,
anticipates the danger, and,
unseen by anyone,
hastens to remove it.
Unconscious of the accident
from which such tender forethought has saved him,
the son will not show any special mark of gratitude for it,
or feel the same love for his father
that he would have,
had he been cured of some grievous wound.
But if he came to learn the whole truth,
would he not love his father all the more?

I am this child.

I am the object of the foreseeing love of a father
who did not send his Son to call the just, but sinners.
He wishes me to love him
because he has forgiven me,
not much
but everything.
He has made me to understand
how he has loved me
with an ineffable love and forethought,
in order that my own love
may reach even unto folly.

I have often heard it said
that an innocent soul
has never loved more than a repentant one.

Let me give lie to these words.

All Through the Day

Our Father did not send his Son
to call the just,
but sinners.

My Day Is Ending

Loving Father,
I am the object of your foreseeing love.

I am one of those sinners
whom you sent your son
to call.

You wish me to love you
because you have forgiven me everything.

Make me understand
that you have loved me
with ineffable love and forethought,
in order that my own love
may reach even unto folly.

Come, then, my loving Father,
you have blessed all my days;
bless me still
as this day ends
and the night begins.

Day Twenty-Four

••••

My Day Begins

For me,
prayer is an uplifting of the heart,
A glance towards heaven,
a cry of gratitude and love
in times of sorrow as well as joy.
It is something noble,
something supernatural,
that expands the soul
and unites it to God.

When my state of spiritual aridity is such
that not a single good thought will come
I repeat very slowly
the Our Father and the Hail Mary,
which suffice to console me,
and provide divine food for my soul.

Apart from the Divine Office,
which in spite of my unworthiness,
is a daily joy,
I have neither the desire
nor the courage
to search through books
for beautiful prayers.

They are so numerous,
that it would only make my head ache,

and besides
each one is lovelier than the next.
Unable either to say them all
or to choose between them,
I do as a child who cannot read would do,
I just say
what I want to say to God
quite simply
and he never fails to understand.

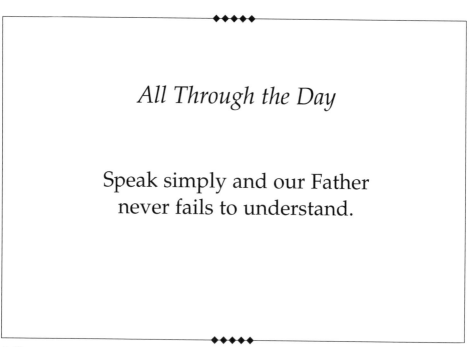

All Through the Day

Speak simply and our Father
never fails to understand.

My Day Is Ending

Loving Father,
the words of others when they pray
may be more beautiful
and more profound,
but I know that I can say to you,
quite simply,
just what I want to say,
even when a single good thought will not come,
and know that you will understand.

I lift up my heart,
I glance toward heaven,
I tell you of my gratitude and love,
in times of sorrow as well as joy.

I feel my soul expand.

I taste the supernatural.

Come, then, my loving Father,
you have blessed all my days;
bless me still
as this day ends
and the night begins.

Day Twenty-Five

❖❖❖❖❖

My Day Begins

Do not let your weakness make you unhappy.
When, in the morning,
you feel no courage or strength
for the practice of virtue,
it is really a time for grace.
It is the time to
"Lay the ax to the foot of the tree."
It is time to rely solely on Jesus.
Life is often burdensome and bitter.
It is hard to begin a day of toil,

especially when
Jesus hides himself from our love.
What is this sweet friend about?
If he sees our anguish
and the burdens that weigh us down,
why does he not come and comfort us?
Have no fear.
He is at our side.
Jesus may hide himself,
but we know that he is there.
Our tears are the only way we have
to prepare ourselves to know him
as he knows himself,
and to become ourselves as God!
If we fall,
an act of love will set it all right.

Jesus will help us
without seeming to do so.
For love can do all things.

The most impossible tasks
can be made to seem easy and sweet.
You know well
that our Lord does not look
so much at the greatness of our actions,
or even at their difficulty,
as at the love with which we do them.

What then do we have to fear?

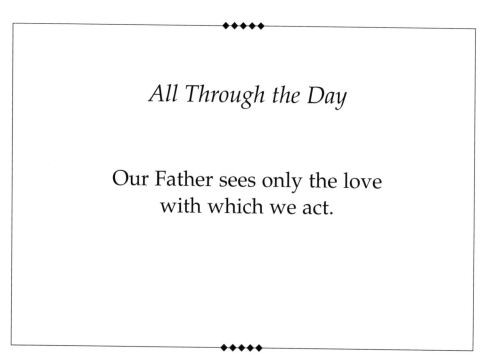

All Through the Day

Our Father sees only the love
with which we act.

My Day Is Ending

Loving Father,
you see my anguish
and the burdens that weigh me down.
Take away my fear.
Be at my side.
I know well
that you do not look
so much at the greatness of my actions,
or even at their difficulty,
as at the love with which I do them.
Why then do I fear?
When I fall,
an act of love will set it all right.
You will help me

without seeming to do so.
For love can do all things.

Come, then, my loving Father,
you have blessed all my days;
bless me still
as this day ends
and the night begins.

Day Twenty-Six

My Day Begins

"We shed tears as we remember Zion,
for how can we sing the songs of the Lord
in a strange land?"

The burden of our song is suffering,
for Jesus offers us a chalice of great bitterness.
Let us not withdraw our lips from it,
but suffer in peace.
He who says peace does not say joy,
at least not a joy that can be felt.

To suffer in peace
it is enough
to will heartily all that our Lord wills.

Do not think that we can find love without suffering.
Indeed it is our very livelihood.
and so precious
that Jesus came down to earth to possess it.
Of course we should like
to suffer generously and nobly;
we should like never to fall.
What an illusion!
What does it matter if I fall at every step?
In that way I realize my weakness,
and my soul's gain is considerable.
My God, you see
how little I am good for,

away from your arms.
If you are willing to bear in peace
the trial of not being pleased with yourself,
you will be offering the Master a home in your heart.
It is true that you will suffer,
because you will be like a stranger in your own home.
But do not be afraid.
The poorer you are,
the more Jesus will love you.
It is better for your soul's growth
to stumble in the night on a stony road and still go on,
than to walk comfortably in the full light of day
on a path carpeted with flowers.

All Through the Day

Love for our Father
does not walk a path
carpeted in flowers.

My Day Is Ending

Loving Father,
it is hard for me to accept
that I cannot find love without suffering,
to understand and accept
that you have promised us
peace, not joy.

Of course I would like
to suffer generously and nobly,
never falling.
What an illusion!
What does it matter if I fall at every step?

To suffer in peace
it is enough

to will heartily all that you will.
It is better for my soul
to stumble in the night on a stony road
and still go on,
than to expect always to walk comfortably
in the full light of day
on a path carpeted with flowers.

Come, then, my loving Father,
you have blessed all my days;
bless me with your peace
as this day ends
and the night begins.

Day Twenty-Seven

◆◆◆◆◆

My Day Begins

Our divine Lord asks
no sacrifice beyond our strength.

At times, it is true,
he makes us taste to the full
the bitterness of the chalice he puts to our lips.
And when he demands the sacrifice
of all that is dearest on earth,
it is impossible
without a very special grace,

not to cry out
as he did during his agony in the garden:
"My Father let this chalice pass from me."
But we must hasten to add as he did:
"Nevertheless, not as I will, but as you will."
It is consoling to remember
that Jesus, "the strong God"
has felt all our weakness
and shuddered at the sight of the bitter chalice—
that very chalice
that he so ardently desired.

A saint has said:
"The greatest honor God can bestow upon a soul
is not to give it great things,
but to ask of it great things."

Was it not
by suffering and death
that God ransomed the world?
The martyrdom of the heart
is not less fruitful
than the shedding of blood.

Have I not, then, good reason
to say that our lot is a beautiful one—
worthy of an apostle of Christ?

All Through the Day

Our Father in his love
will ask of us great things.

My Day Is Ending

Loving Father,
you are the source of great gifts
but you also ask for great sacrifice.
At times, you may ask me to taste to the full
a bitter chalice,
even the sacrifice
of all that is dearest to me on earth.
And though you never ask
for what is beyond my strength,
it is impossible for me
not to cry out
as Jesus did
during his agony in the garden:
"My Father let this chalice pass from me."

But let me never forget to add
as your Son did:
"not as I will,
but as you will,"
for was it not
by suffering and death
that you ransomed the world?

Come, then, my loving Father,
you have blessed all my days;
bless me still
as this day ends
and the night begins.

Day Twenty-Eight

•••••

My Day Begins

I have often thought
that perhaps I owe all the graces
with which I have been blessed
to some little soul
whom I shall know only in heaven.

Some time ago
I was watching the almost imperceptible flicker
of a tiny night light.
One of the sisters came up
and, having lit her own candle in the dying flame,

passed it round
to light the candles of the others,
and the thought came to me:
Who dares glory in her own works?

Just one such faint spark
can set the whole world on fire.
We are so aware of the bright light
of the saints
set high on the church's candlestick,
and we think
we are receiving from them
grace and light.
But from whence
do they borrow their fire?
Very possibly

from the prayers
of some devout and hidden soul
whose inward light
is not apparent to human eyes,
some soul of unrecognized virtue,
and in her own sight, of little worth—
a dying flame!

What mysteries shall we one day see revealed!
For it is God's will
that here below,
we shall give to one another
the heavenly treasures
with which our Father has enriched us.

All Through the Day

Who dares to glory in her own works?

My Day Is Ending

Loving Father,
I ask you as this day ends
to especially bless
all those known and unknown to me
whose lives have ignited and sustained
the fires of faith and love in my soul.

In your wisdom and love
you have joined us together
so that here below
we share with one another
the heavenly treasures
with which you have enriched us.
I dare not take glory in my own works,

for I do not know
from where the fire in my soul comes
or indeed what fires my life is meant to ignite.

Come, then, my loving Father,
who has blessed all my days;
bless me still
and all those with whom I am joined.
Grant to all of us your peace
as this day ends
and the night begins.

Day Twenty-Nine

◆◆◆◆◆

My Day Begins

I love St. Augustine and St. Mary Magdalene,
those souls to whom much was forgiven
because they loved much.
I love their sorrow and affectionate daring.
When I see Mary Magdalene
come forth before all of Simon's guests
to wash with tears her Master's feet,
feet that she is for the first time touching,
I feel that her heart
has fathomed the heart of Jesus,

that abyss of love and mercy.
I feel too that not only was he willing to forgive her,
but willing even
to dispense liberally the favors
of a divine and intimate relationship
and to raise her to the loftiest heights of prayer.

Since I have come to understand
the love of the heart of Jesus,
I confess that all fear has been driven from my heart.
The remembrance of my faults
humbles me,
and helps me never
to rely on my own strength,
which is mere weakness.
More than all, it speaks to me of mercy and love.

When a soul with childlike trust
casts her faults into Love's all-devouring furnace,
how can she escape being utterly consumed?
I know that many saints
have passed their lives
in the practice of amazing penance
for the sake of expiating their sins.
But what of that?
"In my Father's house there are many mansions."
These are the words of Jesus,
and therefore I follow the path he marks out for me.
I try in no way
to be concerned about myself,
and to abandon unreservedly to him
the work he deigns to accomplish in my soul.

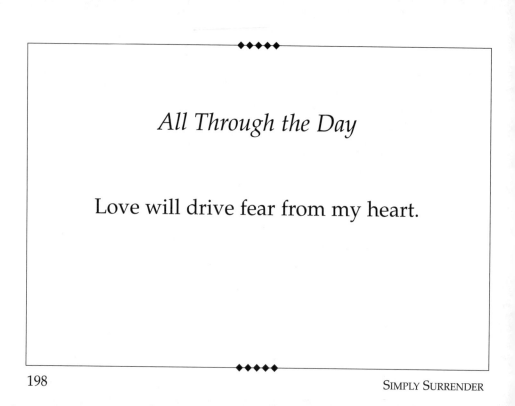

All Through the Day

Love will drive fear from my heart.

SIMPLY SURRENDER

My Day Is Ending

Loving Father,
let me follow with confidence
the path you have marked out for me.
With Thérèse
I try not to be
in any way concerned about myself,
but to abandon myself
unreservedly to you,
so that you can accomplish
your work in me.

With Thérèse's childlike trust
I would like to cast all sins
into the all-devouring furnace of your love,

where they cannot escape being utterly consumed.

I live believing
that your love for me,
my love for you,
will drive fear from my heart

Come, then, my loving Father,
you have blessed all my days;
bless me still
as this day ends
and the night begins.

Day Thirty

◆◆◆◆◆

My Day Begins

I have labored above all to love God,
but it was in loving him
that I discovered the hidden meaning of these words:
"Not everyone who says Lord, Lord,
shall enter the kingdom of heaven,
but he that does the will of my Father."

This will our Lord revealed to me
through the words of his new commandment,
addressed to his apostles at the Last Supper
when he told them:

"Love one another as I have loved you."
I set out to find how he loved his disciples
and I saw that it was not for their natural qualities,
seeing that they were but ignorant men,
whose minds dwelt chiefly on earthly things.
Yet he calls them his friends, his brothers.
He desires to have them close to him
in the kingdom of heaven.
And to open this kingdom to them,
he wills to die on the cross, saying:
"Greater love than this no man has,
that a man lay down his life for his friends."

I understand now
that true charity consists
in bearing all my neighbor's defects,

in not being surprised by their mistakes,
but being edified by their smallest virtues.
Above all I have learned
that charity must not be kept shut up in the heart,
for "no one lights a candle,
and puts it in a hidden place, or under a bushel;
but upon a candlestick,
that they who come in may see the light."
The candle, it seems to me,
represents the charity
that enlightens and gladdens,
not only those who are dearest to us,
but likewise all of our brothers and sisters everywhere.

◆◆◆◆◆

All Through the Day

Greater love no one has
than to lay down one's life
for one's friends.

◆◆◆◆◆

My Day Is Ending

Loving Father,
to enter into your kingdom
it is not enough to come into your presence
as I do now
and speak your name
and vow my love to you.
Words are not enough.
I must do your will
and fulfill your new commandment
to love one another as you have loved us.
Let me not hide your love
in the secret places of my heart,
for no one lights a candle,
and puts it in a hidden place,

nor under a bushel;
but upon a candlestick,
that they who come in may see the light.
My love for you is not complete
until it enlightens and gladdens
not only those who are dearest to me,
but likewise all of my brothers and sisters everywhere.

Come, then, my loving Father,
you have blessed all my days;
bless me still
as this day ends
and the night begins.

One Final Word

This book was created to be nothing more than a gateway—a gateway to the spiritual wisdom of a specific teacher, and a gateway opening on your own spiritual path.

You may decide that Thérèse of Lisieux is someone whose experience of God is one that you wish to follow more closely and deeply, in which case you should get a copy of the entire text of her autobiography and pray it as you have prayed this gateway journey.

You may decide that her experience has not helped you. There are many other teachers. Somewhere there is the right teacher for your own, very special, absolutely unique journey of the spirit. You will find your teacher; you will discover your path.

We would not be searching, as St. Augustine reminds us, if we had not already found.